The Paintings and Drawings of Jan "Flower" Bruegel

Front end paper: *Wagons on a Woodland Path*. Victoria and Albert Museum, London
Back end paper: *Canal Scene*. British Museum, London

Translated from German by
Leonard Mins

Library of Congress Catalog Card Number: 69-12479
Copyright 1968 in West Germany by Verlag M. DuMont Schauberg, Cologne
All rights reserved. No part of the contents of this book may be
reproduced without the written permission of the publishers
Harry N. Abrams, Incorporated, New York

Printed and bound in West Germany

Table of Contents

For Ch. K.

Preface and Acknowledgments

*Every beloved object
is the midpoint of
a paradise.*
Novalis

This book on the art of Jan Bruegel the Elder,[1] called "Flower Bruegel," does not pretend to be a new contribution to Bruegel research. It is deliberately addressed to art-loving laymen, those interested in art and receptive to art. Its outstanding and characteristic examples of this Flemish old-master's art introduce museum and gallery visitors to Rubens' friend and collaborator.

During my study of Jan Bruegel's paintings, both here and abroad, I often had the opportunity of observing the reactions of museum visitors. The receptive ones were not infrequently fascinated by the artistic commitment and the perfection of craftsmanship revealed in the paintings. The delicacy of the craftsmanship often attained the ultimate limits of the technically possible. It is not surprising, therefore, that many spectators could not suppress exclamations of astonishment and admiration at the loving faithfulness with which even the minute details were reproduced. In our book we endeavor to acquaint the reader with this important aspect of Bruegel's work by including enlarged details of several paintings.

Jan Bruegel was quite conscious of the quality of his art, and of his flower paintings in particular. In letters to Cardinal Federigo Borromeo,[2] his most influential patron, he said: "I believe that nothing finer and more painstaking has ever been seen in oil painting"[3] and "that never before have so many rare and diverse flowers been painted nor with such painstaking care."[4]

Only a selection of his works can be printed here, and we shall also have to forego an exposition of the continuous development of style in Jan Bruegel's art. Yet I hope—and I should consider it the best recompense for my labors— to be able to "guide the eye"[5] in Wölfflin's meaning of the phrase by means of descriptions of the pictures and to communicate to the reader some of my own joy in this painter's pictures.

Dr. Ulrich Häussermann helpfully provided the cultural and personal backgrounds of flower painting and flower poetry, particularly for the introductory chapter. I am grateful to him for his contribution.

I am also especially indebted to my kind and deeply revered teacher, Emeritus Prof. Dr. Johannes Wilde, Deputy Director of the Courtauld Institute of Art of the University of London. I also wish to thank Count Antoine Seilern, London, for permission to reproduce the priceless Rubens in his private collection, depicting the family of Jan Bruegel the Elder. Mr. Gipps-Smith, Public Relations Officer, London; Prof. Einar Perman, Upsala; Dr. Paul Boerlin of the Oeffentliche Kunstsammlung, Basel; Mlle. Silvie Béguin of the Louvre, Paris; and the directors of the Prado, Madrid, have rendered invaluable assistance in procuring the illustrative material. I am indebted to Mlle. Béguin, Dr. Friederike Klauner of the Kunsthistorisches Museum, Vienna, and Reverend Chaplain Scholz, Celle, for other valuable suggestions related to the inception of this book.

G. W.-Rh.

The Painter and the Flower

She entices flowers from seeds,
Suns from the firmament.
Schiller

A flower and its picture have in common that they realize and convey a strong positive force. There is a word for this force: pleasure.

This kind of pleasure has the restfulness, the quietness of the flower itself. It is not related to transient humor or boisterous play. If a shadow passes over it, the pleasure retreats into the background, where it continues unnoticed.

What kind of background is active here, what particular impulse is at work? Let us try to explore this question somewhat more closely.

When we look at a picture of a flower, or at the flower itself, memory comes alive. Consciously, subconsciously, or unconsciously, we are in the sphere of untroubled, childlike innocence, intensely colored dreaming and awakening, fairylike quiet.

A concept whose pure meaning has to be rediscovered enters here: heart. The seventeenth-century German hymnist Paul Gerhardt (who was an extraordinary poet despite all later penitent singsong) had reason to begin his song of Paradise with: "Go from my heart and seek joy." For joy that feeds on this—"Look at the beautiful garden's ornaments ... narcissus and tulip, fairer than Solomon's silk"—is, in a precise sense, joy of the heart.

Naturally enough, flower poets and flower painters have always had a special, "inspired" relationship with this concept. They take the subject of their art, more or less literally, from external nature. They take the power to shape the object into a meaningful picture from that other, deep-lying impulse.

The intuitive knowledge that guides the pen or the brush is also the source of folk myths. Seldom or never is it intellectual. Novalis, the Romantic poet, suggests it is "not the colors ... that enrapture us so much in the spring. It is the still, prophetic spirit" that speaks through the flowers, "the presentiment of higher eternal blossoms and fruits."

Art, which began as magic, spells, and incantations, still contains a residue of incantation in its masterpieces.

Whether a loving queen offers her consort a branch of mandrake as a magical love gift in an Egyptian wall painting, or Chagall's women carry the fairy-tale nosegay, or the Gothic *Madonna in the Strawberries* (Fig. 1) gives the Child the mystical blessed rose in a ritual gesture, or the Expressionist painter Paula Modersohn-Becker sees her own austere figure holding a flower—the flower is always something more than a decoration, a color value.

It is always "charged." It conveys strength, significance, and essence. The link to the intuitive layer differs from one artist to another, of course. The impelling motivation is always the same (the Greeks called it *Mnemosyne*, "Memory"), though the mode of understanding, the "refraction," is different.

The primeval symbolism of a flower in art may be differentiated into five types, or shades of meaning, whose boundaries are often indistinct. Developments since the sixteenth century have blurred the differences and diluted many of the sources but have never involved any change in its necessary links to its "occult" source. These types, so full of discrete meaning no matter how closely they are related, are: meditation image, signum (symbol), talisman, sacrifice, and medicine.

The Hindu concept of the thousand-petaled lotus, depicted in infinite variations (often as the throne of Buddha), is a meditation image. It is based on the opening of the mind's eye, experienced in the visionary glow *(tapas)*, which opens up like a lotus *(budh,* "awakening")—the blossom as an expression of the interior fire. Eastern representations of the lotus often turn, consequently, into the idea of the flower as a sacrifice. The early Chinese and Japanese flower poems and flower paintings, rooted in the Zen movement, must also be regarded as meditation images.

The flowers mentioned in fairy tales are also meditation images. In the Grimm fairy tale, Joringel, whose betrothed Jorinda is a prisoner in an enchanted cage, dreams that he finds a blood-red flower, with a beautiful large pearl at its center, and everything he touches with the flower is freed of enchantment. Here the flower has a truly visionary significance. The flower, in its meditative meaning of awakening and illumination, loosens all fetters.

Other fairy tales tell of the flower with which the secret casket can be opened ("perceived" is the actual word used); a light touch suffices, and the casket springs open with a thin, clear tinkle. Here the casket is Memory, the heart.

Plant names such as "tree of heaven" and "forget-me-not" originated in such folklore.

The flower is a meditation image in the cryptic words of German mystics, such as in the descriptions by St. Hildegard, Mechtild, Tauler, and Suso. Thus in Tauler's quiet song "A Laden Ship Is Coming," we find:

> Upon the softly rolling waves,
> A little bark is wafted near.
> It bears a splendid, royal gift—
> Our heavenly queen.
>
> Mary, thou rose sublime,
> Fortune be with thee for aye.
> Thou fairest snowdrop,
> Keep us all by sin unstained.

Grünewald is in this mystical tradition when he has three dark-red roses (an allusion to the celebrated *rosa mystica*) bloom close to the Mother of God in his *Nativity* from the Isenheim Altar. Some of the rose petals touch the Virgin's blond hair. In this work, where all objects are translated into a single flow of events in accord with the master's inspired temperament, the rose constitutes a secret resting point, cloaked in gossamer poetry.

It is a meditation image, drawn from the same source as when Hölderlin, unacquainted with the medieval doctrine of signatures, writes in one of his last apocalyptic hymns:

> As a sign of love
> The earth is dyed with violet hue.

The violet is the flower of humility (*humilitatis viola*, St. Jerome), meditatively delicate and pious as shown by Stefan Lochner in the Virgin's hand (Fig. IV).

Then, too, it is a meditation image when the old sagas tell of the flower growing out of a corpse's mouth. His soul lives on, transmuted into color and fragrance. About 1275, Albrecht von Scharffenberg told of two vines that issued from the graves of the lovers Sigune and Schionatulander:

> Green as Archmardi the vines from both mouths sprouted,
> Mountain-high they twined together,
> And their blossoms faded never.

I *Sheaf of Flowers in a Wooden Bucket ("Crown Imperial Bouquet")*. Detail of Frontispiece

Flower meditation evolved into the mystical picture of Paradise. The absolutely pure garden, where all the flowers of the year bloom simultaneously and all the world's animals live together timelessly without fear under a blessed spell—found in the myths of all peoples—had its counterpart in the magic flower garden of Klingsor the magician in the legend of Parsifal. One variant of the mystical Paradise is the apocalyptic City of Jerusalem; Suso described the splendor of the heavenly city, how it "glitters from afar with paved gold, radiates with noble daisies, inlaid with precious stones, clear as crystal, reflecting red roses, white lilies, and all sorts of living flowers."

The celebrated mosaic in the apse of San Apollinare in Classe near Ravenna (consecrated in 549) is an early pinnacle of flower portrayal. St. Apollinaris, as a shepherd, stands imparting his blessing in a landscape of Paradise built up of childlike pious images: white lambs, white lilies, red roses, and delicate daisies adorn the fairylike meadow.

In the Middle Ages artists painted and poets wrote about the "enclosed garden" of the Virgin Mary. This notion goes back to Solomon's "Song of Songs." A master of the Upper Rhine School pictures this "enclosed garden" with exquisite detail and charm (Fig. III). The flowers of the entire year bloom alongside one another in truly paradisiacal fashion. Clockwise from the top left, they include: mullein pink, stock, iris, hollyhock, lily, primrose, columbine, strawberry, peony, and lily of the valley. At the hem of Mary's skirt there are violets, primroses, and snowdrops.[6]

The mystical spectacle is executed here with almost affectionate accuracy, with the Middle Ages' pleasure in extended narrative that we find in the great epics. A timeless pleasure in being present is transmitted to the viewer— pleasure in the "ornaments of the beautiful gardens."

The other types—the flower as signum, as talisman, as sacrifice, and as medicine—are also rooted in the meditation image, of course. But in them the flower has a special significance, whereas meaning grew out of the flower itself in the meditation image. As meditation the "idea" of the flower was vague and had many meanings. Here it is comprehended and defined.

Where enlightened knowledge was lacking there was a searching desire to classify the closed book of the laws of life according to new aspects. New guiding principles were sought in order to discover the forces that operated through plants. Endeavors to decipher nature as if it were runic writing culminate in the doctrine of signatures— nourished by ancient myths, extended and differentiated by Arabic and Semitic traditions, and expanded by scientific research.

In medieval pictures a plant, regarded as a cipher, often embodied the explanation of the picture's content. The language of flowers revealed the characters, events, and emotions portrayed in the picture. Diligent erudition was associated with pious detail.

Flowers almost always have a purely symbolic value in the medieval epic (especially in the works of Wolfram von Eschenbach), but most of all where they are heraldic: on shields, helmets, and banners. Symbolic meaning of a similarly rigorous nature is found in, say, the well-known minnesinger portraits of the Manasse manuscript. The delicate red and yellow flowers that cover air and earth around the meditating *Herr Heinrich von Veldecke*, for example, indicate the nature and imagination of this poet.

Similarly compelling is the flower symbolism of the Gobelin tapestries, and especially the extraordinarily fine pomegranate pattern in the Upper Rhenish tapestries *(Minneteppiche)* woven around 1430 (Basel, Frankfort, and Sigmaringen). The figures and the emblematic background are so interwoven here that they become almost indistinguishable.

In this sense flowers are symbols in medieval pictures, but we often find an echo of the therapeutic effect of plants as well.

II *Little Bouquet in a Clay Jar ("Iris Bouquet")*. Panel, $20^1/_8 \times 15^3/_4''$

The individual plant should not be interpreted too pedantically. Still, we are struck by the stereotyped attribution of certain "leading flowers" to certain themes in a picture. This often suggests a pregnant symbolic interpretation.

The Master of Flémalle surely had this code in mind when he painted the flowers surrounding the robe of his *St. Veronica* (Fig. II). The saint stands "rooted" in the growth of the "holy herb." Reading from left to right, we see: plantain, lily of the valley, campion, buttercup, dead nettle, dandelion, lungwort, agrimony, and borage.[7]

A flower as symbol is rarely a flower as talisman, though a flower as talisman is always a flower as signum as well.

Whenever plants are invoked magically—as protection, as healing energy, or as an elixir of immortality—they are talismans.

In the Hindu *Atharva-Veda* (c. 1000 B.C.) the efficacious murmuring of many spells depended on the simultaneous employment of sacred herbs and flowers. The sacred herb was part of the rites of primitive religions (sacrifice, initiation, and purification). The magic power of eternal recurrence inherent in plants was regarded as a pledge and was invoked to strengthen man's vitality and protect it as with a charm.

"There is hardly any limit to the employment of herbs in amulets. They were consecrated in church, worn in bunches, capsules, and little bags, sewed into clothing, and kept in furniture and rooms."[8]

One of the countless incantations that were taken for granted in folklore well into the nineteenth century was the "Three-Flower Spell."[9] The rose spell is said to be the oldest form; the lily spell may be a later variant. Both were employed as styptic charms. Here is a sixteenth-century example:

Three roses grow as if
From our Lord God's heart.
One is His grace,
Two, His humility,
Three, His good will,
Blood—stand thou still.

Here the flower was not supposed to act as a medicine in the material sense, but rather as a "healing herb" in the occult sense.

The flower possessed a similar significance as a spell in votive paintings and stained-glass medallions, which persisted well into the nineteenth century. These direct, childlike, devout pictures always had their radiant flower, usually as large as the figure of God or the saint himself. The flower reinforced the talismanic power of the holy picture.

The chicory depicted by the Master of the Augustine Altar (Fig. VI) has the significance of a purely magical plant. In J. Schroeder's *Medicin-Chymischen höchste kostbahren Artzneyschatz* ("Most Precious Hoard of Chemical-Medical Medicines") of 1693, this flower is reputed to possess the secret effect of "protecting against all sorts of puncture wounds." The significance of the chicory as a talisman is clearly revealed at the feet of the martyred St. Sebastian.

The significance of a flower as a sacrifice is a bit more subtle.

The plant is resolved into its elements—the tree into its branches, leaves, blossoms, and fruits; and the flower into its petals, its essential oil, and its fragrance. The blessings thus sacrificed invoked the blessings of the Deity.

This is the background of the age-old offerings of perfumes and incense, from the rustic smoking-out of stable and farmyard for protection against evil spirits to the incense of the Mass, rising like the breath of prayer.

The Delphic priestess, entranced by holy vapors, uttered oracles; the medicine man of the American Indians, transported into ecstasy by smoke rising from the burnt offering, cured the sick. Hardly any present-day smoker is conscious of the sacrificial significance of his behavior, which was originally a ritual act.

The interest of the peoples of antiquity and the Orient in cultivating and dealing in spices is primarily attributable to this magical thinking, and only later to the special desire for refined gastronomic pleasure.

III *Little Bouquet in a Clay Jar* (*"Iris Bouquet"*). Detail of colorplate II

The palm offering is age-old and still very much alive in the Catholic South of Germany: palm branches (or the flowering branches of the meadow) are spread in the path of the Saviour, Who symbolically walks through the streets. Subjects strewed petals of roses and violets before their princesses, lovers did the same for their ladies, as did those saying their prayers to the Deity.

Paul Gerhardt, going back to an old tradition, wrote:

> I am going to gather flowers
> So that my Saviour's couch
> Is covered with lovely violets.

The irises, lilies, and columbines seen in the detail from Hugo van der Goes' Portinari Altar (Fig. V) are symbolic of sacrifice, while the violets—the flower of humility—scattered below them (not visible in the detail reproduced here) are a reminder of Christ's lowly birth. All these flowers imply mankind's adoration of Jesus as well as His sacrifice, predestined at His Nativity. Here, as in the scent offerings, the aura of joy has a quite singular, intimate note.

The occult vision of the flaming flower, which is repeated in many traditions, is probably another instance of sacrifice.

Medicine was closely related to the doctrine of signatures in ancient and medieval civilizations, much more self-evidently than today. Now only a few physicians, who are usually ridiculed, include the aspect of plant shape in their therapeutic practice.

Paracelsus considered the shape of a plant to be a key to its therapeutic potency, though he presupposed a differentiated mastery of such knowledge. "By *chiromantiam, physiognomiam,* and *magiam* art it is possible to recognize the property and virtue of every herb and root from its outward appearance, by its *signatis,* its shape, form, and color" (c. 1530).

The unusual association of painter and physician is an old tradition. St. Luke was the patron of the medieval confraternities of painters and woodcarvers. (Jan Bruegel the Elder headed the Guild of St. Luke in Antwerp.) Legend has it that St. Luke was a painter and physician.

This kind of therapeutic painting is seen most clearly in Grünewald. In fact, critics have referred to "Grünewald's medical science."[10]

It is not pride in abstract botanical knowledge that Grünewald displays in his highly lyrical and astonishingly exact paintings of plants, but rather a veiled concern with the healing art. This may be traced, for example, in his *St. Elizabeth* (1509). The calling of the saint, known as a nurse of the poor and the sick, is set forth as it were by the medicinal herbs growing at her feet. The common mallow, an old folk remedy having a resolving, demulcent action, grows on an upright stalk. Crosswise beneath it there is the styptic agrimony. Galium verum, a pediatric remedy and diuretic, winds inconspicuously among the mallow leaves, rising upward toward the right.

No one thinks of a genius like Grünewald as a literal herbalist. He saw the curative "soul" of the plant and translated it into a blazing line. This is what makes Grünewald's flowers so brilliant, so delicate, so spiritual. The body of the plant sways in a movement "in which matter seems to lose its consistency."[11]

We shall have to be brief in outlining the basic symbolism of flowers in art and its various nuances.

As these brief remarks indicate, the flower painting of antiquity and the Middle Ages was always spiritually burdened. It was governed by, moved by, and filled with an inner meaning.

Nor did spiritually interpretative vision end with the Renaissance. The artists continued to create symbols, but the "apprehending," realistic eye was opened alongside the prescient one.

I UPPER RHINE MASTER   Madonna in the Strawberries
1410–1420

II MASTER OF FLEMALLE
(active about 1406–1444)   St. Veronica

III UPPER RHINE SCHOOL   Paradise Garden
About 1410

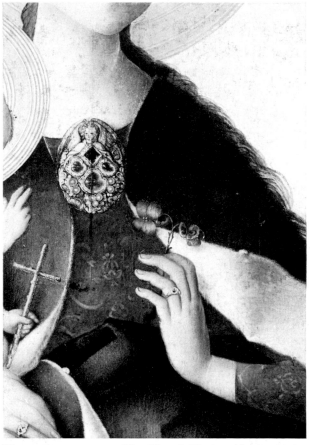

IV STEFAN LOCHNER The Blessed Virgin with the Violet
    (detail) About 1445

V HUGO VAN DER GOES Adoration of the Shepherds (detail) About 1473–1475

VI MASTER OF THE AUGUSTINE ALTAR Martyrdom of St. Sebastian 1487

VII GERARD DAVID Baptism of Christ 1503–1508

VIII   PIETER BRUEGEL   Autumn (The Return of the Herd)   1565
IX   PIETER BRUEGEL   The Parable of the Blind   1568

X PIETER BRUEGEL Two Rabbis About 1563/64

XI Contemporary engraving of Pieter Bruegel

XII JAN BRUEGEL THE YOUNGER The Tower by the Sea 1642

What is important is that we cannot simply expunge our inheritance from this zone. Elements of the meditation image, of the doctrine of signatures, of magic, of the old *materia medica* are still alive. Merely the rigid bond between a plant's image and its occult meaning has been severed.

Flowers and pleasure in flowers became separate entities. But a hasty conclusion that the flower is a discovery of the Renaissance[12] is both facile and false. The Renaissance regarded flowers, like the rest of the universe, in another aspect, in another light. The Renaissance invented the telescope and the microscope; it discovered the structure of the macrocosmos and the microcosmos. The plant was part of this microcosmos. The English scientist John Gerard[13] was the first botanist to employ a magnifying glass. As if with secret pride, Jan Bruegel has placed a magnifying glass on the table in the foreground of his unusual painting *The Sense of Sight* (plate 10).

Botany rapidly developed as an exact science, especially in Western Europe. One of the standard works is the *Rarorum Plantorum Historia* by Charles de l'Escluse, professor in Leyden (1601). The plant became an object of the measuring, counting, differentiating, and cataloguing mind.

Without implying anything derogatory, we should have to say that flowers were a Renaissance fashion, or rather one of its fashions. What were most pleasing were uncommon flowers, those coming from far away. We owe some of our most beautiful garden flowers to this Renaissance liking for the universal. The flowers of the medieval monastery garden—roses, lilies, carnations, irises, violets, columbines, lilies of the valley, peonies, and wallflowers—were joined after 1550 by "Turkish" flowers, which reached the West via Vienna—tulips, ranunculuses, fritillaries, hyacinths, and calendulas. The flowers coming from the newly discovered "India" (Central America)—marigolds, nasturtiums, and sunflowers—evoked the liveliest interest, however.

Bringing back flower cuttings and bulbs from far-off countries to display an exotic treasure in one's garden was proof of a particularly high level of culture. A flower market was held every year in Frankfort, where the latest acquisitions were exchanged with learned enthusiasm. It was considered good breeding in the British and Dutch officers' corps to be concerned with botanical problems. The famous tulipomania in Holland was so extreme as to be the ruin of several great fortunes.

The great botanical gardens were laid out as "laboratories" for the new science. Their precursor was the monastery garden of the Middle Ages, in which sacred herbs and medicinal plants were cultivated. The first "medicinal garden" arose in Italy about 1300. After botany had been divorced from medicine, every large university obtained its own botanical garden. The first one was established in Padua in 1543, followed by Leyden in 1577, Leipzig in 1580, Paris in 1597, and Montpellier in 1598.

Science's new analytical approach to flowers slowly permeated art as well. To be sure, scientific analysis can never direct art, but it can provide exact dimensions and distinct laws of structure. It can give the artist a higher degree of detached awareness.

In the Renaissance, the artist for the first time took the step of making the flower the subject of his picture. Only in the Far East was there any independent flower painting prior to the sixteenth century.

The nature studies of the great artists may serve as examples of anatomical awareness of the plant's shape. In Dürer's classic watercolors (violets, columbines, Turk's-cap lilies, celandines, etc.) the texture, color, form, and structural laws of the plant are reproduced with faithful naturalistic precision. Leonardo da Vinci subtly depicted the development of plants as they grow, their "atmosphere," in his botanical sketches.

We are primarily interested, however, in the developments in the Low Countries. The early painters of the Low Countries exhibited an increasingly mature density and objective repleteness, almost a static approach, in depicting nature. In Gerard David's solemnly placid and very beautiful *Baptism of Christ* (Fig. VII), the artist took his time to paint flowers in a reflective style. Flower painting as such did not exist in the Low Countries before 1600. Carel van

Mander, a contemporary chronicler of art, traces it back to the early pioneers Ludwig Jan van der Bosch and Pieter Coecke van Aelst (both prior to 1550). We possess none of their paintings, however. A work by Ludger tom Ring the Younger (1562) is the earliest known picture with a vase of flowers as its subject.

Jan Bruegel the Elder and his most important pupil, Daniel Seghers, are the principal representatives of the first-generation Low Country flower painters. Jan's first dated flower piece bears the date of 1608.

The ritually rigorous composition of the picture is painted with the fineness of a miniature. An innocent realism, related to that of the early Low Country painters, is combined with the "enthusiastic curiosity of a child"[14] to find, to collect, and to display. The subject, studied with anatomical accuracy, exhibits an ethereal atmosphere, mostly that of an ideal peace. The flower, which is apprehended quite materialistically, seems nevertheless to be bathed in another, otherworldly light.

These brief remarks will suffice for the time being. Let us glance at subsequent developments. The second generation dissolved the rigorous form in lighter movement. Jan Davidsz de Heem, in particular, who represents this generation most distinctly, had the strength for reflection and for a broad elegance. The third generation (Jan van Huysum, Rachel Ruysch, and others) began to reach for a delicate, very colorful "impressionism."

Jan Bruegel the Elder, the subject of this book, was not a genius like his father, "pas un créateur."[15] He did not have the grand vision. He was an intimate painter, who perfected the nuance.

His contemporaries regarded his paintings as marvels.[16] Jan was hardly modest himself in praising his own ability. "I leave it to the judgment of Your Lordship whether these flowers do not surpass gold and jewels," he wrote to Cardinal Borromeo in 1606.[17] Cornelis de Bie, the Baroque art chronicler, actually placed him at the "summit of art" (1661). What they most admired in Jan was his mastery of minute detail, his fascinating ability to make the tiniest concealed object glow. This is the key to his remarkable success.

Jan Bruegel the Elder owes his poetic nickname "Flower Bruegel" to his flower paintings, although the flower pieces of his that have survived are comparatively few in number, compared to those of other flower painters, such as his pupil Daniel Seghers, the Dutchman Jan Davidsz de Heem, and others. In view of the high regard enjoyed by Bruegel during his own lifetime it is hard to believe that the bulk of his work has been lost.

It is difficult to say whether his contemporaries, in giving him that sobriquet, simply wanted to distinguish him from "Peasant Bruegel" and "Hell Bruegel." This predicate might well have served as a mark of distinction for the first qualified flower painter in the history of Western art.

Of course there are other aspects of his flower paintings' timeless significance, and we shall confine our attention to them for the moment. One of the most important aspects is the simplicity of his composition. He was not born with it; he had to work it out himself. The painting of flowers is the work of the mature Jan. This simplicity gives his works, especially the flower pieces proper, a tranquil strength.

This often cultish tranquillity is reinforced by the airiness of drawing and color. Then there is that strange light filling his pictures, which flows around all forms with hardly any shadow. This light is not harsh, but bright as crystal.

The tranquillity, delicacy, and light combine to make Jan's flower pieces look somewhat unearthly, for all their exact realism.

The remarkable, "false" juxtaposition of flowers of all seasons has often been interpreted as evidence of purely botanical thinking. It is not the language of science that speaks in Jan's flower pieces, however. With all their sobriety, they possess a certain magic.

Paradise was the place where all the flowers of the year bloomed simultaneously. The new scientific thought of the Renaissance did not simply sweep away the dream of Paradise, one of mankind's ancient myths; the dream was merely "transposed."

IV *Little Bouquet in a Clay Jar ("Iris Bouquet").* Detail of colorplate II

The Renaissance botanical garden was designed as a research institution, but it was also an oasis, a paradise as perfect as science could make it. The flower mania of the Renaissance is considered to have been an enthusiasm for cataloguing, but it was also the transfigured survival of the dream of the "enclosed garden."

Jan is also called "Paradise Bruegel," not only because he painted several delightful paradisiacal landscapes, but also because he possessed a sort of "fairy sight."

To begin with, this sight of his was guided by an extremely earnest concern for the anatomical thinking of his time. The painter obeyed the laws of nature with loving conscientiousness: "Flowers, all of them painted after nature: in this picture I have painted everything that I am able to do. I believe that never before have so many rare and diverse flowers been painted and with such painstaking care."[18]

But what he studied, observed, reproduced, and shaped "with such painstaking care" was not listed species by species as in a catalogue; he built up to a new, unreal unity. The artist's childlike, yet knowing, innocence felt its way toward a paradisiacal world. The anatomically accurate, correct flower was dipped in another, magical light. The old institution of signum and talisman, sacrifice and medicament, far from forgotten, lingered on secretly.

An intact world that is full of joy, a "child's joy,"[19] is what makes Jan Bruegel's flowers ageless.

The Bruegel Family of Painters

Born to see,
Appointed to observe.
Goethe

Pieter the Elder was to the Bruegel family of painters what Johann Sebastian was to the Bach family of musicians and Peter of Gmünd was to the Parler family of architects: the bearer of the great intuition.

Pieter Bruegel the Elder, the ancestor of the family, was the genius by European standards among the Bruegels. The freshness of his vision, his fanatical veracity, the rhythm of his composition, and his breadth of line were equaled by none of his descendants.

Pieter was probably born before 1525, supposedly in Breda (searching for a birthplace named Bruegel is a futile endeavor). He was taught painting by Pieter Coecke van Aelst. Many years later Pieter married his teacher's daughter.

Pieter had the shortest life of all the painters that bore the Bruegel name, which accorded with the temperament of his works. He painted most of his marvelous oeuvre in the space of some ten years, and died in Brussels at the age of about forty-five.

His nickname "Peasant Bruegel" is somewhat misleading. Pieter was a learned Humanist. The old Flemish nickname, "Viezen-Bruegel," a word with two meanings, is more to the point. It means "Dung Bruegel" or "Ribald Bruegel." He was also called "Per den Drol," or "Peter the Fool."

These nicknames suggest the master's extreme mercilessness, realism, and dry humor. His bluntness and his wittiness were based on a deliberately unacademic boldness in seeing things.

Hieronymus Bosch, whom Pieter resembled in many ways, recorded his fantasies with fiery seriousness and absoluteness, while Pieter introduced a certain coolness. His view was more objective. Relaxed and with humor as warmhearted as it was sharp, he painted what he saw without prettifying it.

What is striking in his language is its directness. Pieter never repeated himself, because he created out of his spontaneous seeing of the truth; he apprehended events. What Pieter always painted was activity.

The drawing *Two Rabbis* (Fig. X) exhibits the master's splendidly astringent eye and his stubborn line, while the painting *Autumn* (Fig. VIII) is an example of the broad style of his later landscapes. A few strong lines compose the picture; two diagonals cut the background. Restful areas (at the center and top left of the painting) balance the wealth of movement (the herd passing toward the left, the clouds passing toward the right). Severe lines (the rocks and bare trees) bind the rich colors together.

Bertolt Brecht said of Pieter Bruegel that the genius of this painter lay in the fact that "in him tragedy itself contains comedy, and his comedy has something tragic." This singular feature (which is related to alienation in modern drama) is seen most clearly in Pieter's last works. *The Parable of the Blind* (Fig. IX) is one of these rather uncanny paintings. The verse is Matthew 15 : 14—"And if the blind lead the blind, both shall fall into the ditch." The column of groping men descends with suggested inevitability in a single diagonal that suddenly drops in a sharp curve. The mature Bruegel—who could scarcely have collated this plethora of phenomena as a youth—here employs only a few piercing symbols: the blindmen's way is roadless; the huge blindmen's canes become impediments; the leader's hurdy-gurdy (the most monotonous of instruments) slips out of his hands; the empty white eyes are blindly lifted toward heaven; the masklike faces are drawn in deathly senselessness. In the background, as a touch of mockery, or perhaps from earnestness, the untouched idyl of a church stands against a pallid sky.

This is a harsh language, which presupposes strength—in the painter and in the spectator—and a dismayingly modern language.

Such intensity of inspiration did not persist for long. The sons of Pieter the Elder tried hard to carry on the work of their great father, but both of them slipped into smoother, academic painting. What was radical—his true freedom—was lost. It would be wrong to overlook this.

Pieter Bruegel the Younger, "Peasant Bruegel's" first-born son, was born five years before his father died. Jan Bruegel the Elder was born one year before his father died. Thus neither of them could have benefited from their father's guidance. They encountered him only in his works.

No doubt challenged by their father's early death, they learned, from their encounter with his works, the painter's eye, the spiritual world, creative commitment, and countless individual traits of the craftsman and artist.

Pieter the Younger was greatly indebted to his father. Some of his works are merely freer copies of his father's paintings. The nickname "Hell Bruegel," which is sometimes used to distinguish the younger Pieter from the elder one, misses the mark. Pieter the Younger did create many hobgoblin scenes and did paint fires and grotesque peasant heads, but his strength lay in portraitlike distinctions between faces, rather than in a unique view of demonic traits. Solid composition was his métier rather than major inventions.

Jan, Pieter's second son, however, has a style that is decidedly his own. The term "Flower Bruegel" refers to his flower paintings, which made him famous, although the term also tells us something about Jan himself. The delicate, painstaking style of his painting is evidence of his love of flowers. His old Flemish nickname is "Fluweelen-Bruegel," which means "Velvet Bruegel." The superficial, somewhat far-fetched interpretation of this name associates it with Jan's liking for sumptuously draped velvet and silk clothing, but it is more likely that the term refers to Jan's velvety brush strokes. The nickname "Velvet Bruegel" is extremely different from his father's "Viezen-Bruegel," a contrast between cool acuity and velvetlike gentleness.

The faces of the father and his son show the differences in their natures (Fig. XI and plate 1). Both have the same strong nose, the same heavy eyebrows that imply keen observation, and the same deep point of concentration just above the nose (more striking in Pieter than in Jan). The father, however, has the steep, almost "craggy" forehead of an intellectual, while the son's has a more harmonious appearance. The father's cheeks have something hard about them, while the son's are full of feeling. The father looks stern and unassuming, while the son's face exhibits distinction and relaxation. (We shall not comment on the impressive power of Rubens' masterpiece here.)

Everything indicates that something other than his paternal heredity was at work in Jan. For one thing Jan's mother was the daughter of a painter and his painter wife. Her father, Pieter Coecke van Aelst, was "Peasant Bruegel's" teacher. This man, Jan's grandfather, must have been highly cultured, as well as a thoroughly well-bred scholar, architect, and painter. He translated the architectural treatises of Vitruvius and Serlio into Flemish, published a book on Turkish costumes, and illustrated these books with drawings that manifest a high degree of graphic competence. Carel van Mander says he was a painter of flowers, but none of these works is known.

Nor do we possess any documents on the more important line of his grandmother, Marie Bessemers (Mayken Verhulst). Mayken, Pieter Coecke's last wife, survived her husband by fifty years and was the decisive factor in the

V *Bouquet in a Blue Vase ("Tulip Bouquet"). Detail of plate 2*

development of little Jan, who had lost his father before his first birthday. Mayken had a high reputation as a miniaturist in Flanders, and she taught Jan the art of watercolor.

This is the source of the "remarkable transparency"[20] that his colors have always preserved, and of his miniaturist's manner of seeing and composition. Throughout his career Jan always "paid more attention to detail than to the whole."[21] The "velvety" delicacy of line that is characteristic of Jan's paintings is presumably attributable to his grandmother's tradition.

The contemporary background sheds a clear light on Jan's life. His childhood was overshadowed by the terrors of the Inquisition. The Spaniards' forced reimposition of Catholicism in the Low Countries cost some six thousand lives in the bloody year 1566 alone. A national confederacy founded by Calvinist noblemen grew rapidly, and on May 5, 1566, it peremptorily demanded that the terror end. The growth of popular unrest paralleled the subversive underground activity of the Gueux (the "Beggars"); political anarchy spread rapidly. The suppressed longing for freedom broke out in a fanatically blind and unfortunate smashing of images, which was pitilessly crushed by Spain's mercenaries. The Duke of Alba's Council of Troubles, popularly called the "Council of Blood," raised the persecution of the Protestants to new, Renaissance-like, heights. It was only under the more moderate ruler Archduke Albert and his consort Isabella that Flanders regained some tranquillity and freedom.

The blossoming artistic life of the time seems almost incomprehensible against this ghastly background. As a matter of fact, some 360 painters and sculptors were active in Antwerp in 1550. There was a thriving trade in works of art; the guilds held a market in pictures on the Kerksplaats in front of the cathedral. Shiploads of art works were sent to Spain; every day five thousand dealers fixed prices; paintings were sold "like grain on the stalk," sometimes even before they were painted.

Jan Bruegel the Elder was born in 1568. He went to school in Antwerp and was taught to paint by Pieter Goetkind and perhaps by the more mature Gillis van Coninxloo.[22] At the age of twenty-one Jan began his travels, which took him via Cologne to Rome.

In Rome he came upon the art of Paul Bril, who was doing heroic landscapes possessing a disciplined, temperamental rhythm, and in Rome he also found his most loyal patron, Cardinal Borromeo,[23] who admired Jan's art as if it were a miracle. The Cardinal thought that what Jan painted had the "lightness of nature itself" *(facilitas sicuti naturae)*, which was the highest praise at the time.

After traveling about for six years, Jan returned home and settled in Antwerp. At the age of thirty he married Isabella Jode, daughter of a copperplate engraver. Their only child was the painter Jan Bruegel the Younger. Two years after Isabella's death (1603) he married Catharina van Marienberghe, who bore him eight more children.

Jan painted almost nothing but landscapes at the beginning of his career, turning to flower pieces later. In contrast to the daring art of Pieter, his father, which was esteemed somewhat as a sort of peasant jest, Jan's art came closer to the Mannerist taste of his time. Jan collected the highest honors and possessions; he soon rose to be dean of the artists' guild, and owned five houses by the time he was fifty. He painted his way into the good graces of the archducal pair, Albert and Isabella, who granted him privileges of all sorts: remission of taxes, exemption from the payment of duty on paintings shipped abroad, and finally the right to study rare plants and animals in the botanical and zoological gardens of their palace. In 1623 he was accorded the honor of having the Archduchess and Cardinal Borromeo serve as the godparents of his youngest daughter, Clara-Eugenia. When Jan Bruegel and three of his children succumbed to cholera, Rubens wrote his friend's epitaph.

Jan left two sons who were talented painters: Jan the Younger, born of his first marriage, and Ambrosius, born of his second. Jan Bruegel the Younger devotedly followed his father's guidance and continued his work, though it was somewhat more dry, more bourgeois (Fig. XII). Because father and son employed the same signature, many of

Blumenschale
Bowl with Flowers
British Museum, London

...dien zum Irdischen Paradies
...arious studies for a picture of
the Terrestrial Paradise
British Museum, London

*Wagen auf der
Landstraße
Landscape with
travelling Waggo*
on a Road
British Museum
London

*Flußlandschaft
River Landscape*
Ehemalige Staa
Museen, Berlin,
Kupferstichkabi

Landstraße im Wald
A Woodland Road
Ehemalige Staatliche
Museen, Berlin,
Kupferstichkabinett

Dorfstraße
Village Street
British Museum,
London

Pferdekarren und Planwagen auf einer Landstraße   *Waggon and cart in a Roadway*   Victoria and Albert Museum, London

their works are hard to distinguish exactly. The son was also proud that his subjects were "all true to life"; he skillfully combined art with business and sold a great deal, mostly to Spain as his father had done.

Ambrosius had a more graceful style. He composed charming landscapes, often drawing on the treasures of his grandfather, "Peasant Bruegel," but he transformed the great mythic heritage into the idyllic.

Jan's daughter Paschasia married the painter Hieronymus van Kessel; their son, Jan van Kessel, was a painter of likable small paintings.

Jan's daughter Anna married the unusual genre painter David Teniers the Younger, known for his frank narratives.

Abraham was the outstanding son of Jan the Younger. He moved to Italy when he was thirty-eight, married Angela Borani, an Italian, and lived the rest of his life as Abramo Brugolo in Naples. His academic style, which characterized his highly interesting, exotic flower pieces and fruit still lifes, is somewhat cool and decorative for all the depth of its chiaroscuro.

VI *Bouquet ("Lily Bouquet")*. Detail of plate 4

Flower Bruegel

As we have said, Jan Bruegel the Elder began to paint flowers late in life. After 1610 flowers became his major creative interest, and he reached his zenith toward 1615. Most of his flower pieces (many of which cannot be dated exactly) must have been painted between 1610 and 1621.

Thus the flower still life is the master's mature work. That is, when we begin with the flower pieces we survey his art from its final stage.

Everything that Jan Bruegel was capable of—his clarity, his knowledge of light and beauty, his delicacy and his understanding, as well as the scope of his imagination—is perfectly visible here.

Flower still lifes were ideally suited to concentrate all of Jan's talents, developing them to the fullest. In the flower pieces he attained the simplicity that is often lacking in his early work. It is this splendid simplicity that makes it possible to distinguish his flower pieces from all subsequent ones.

The clearly proportioned mass in the *Little Bouquet in a Clay Jar* (colorplate II) is placed at the center of the picture. The colors follow the conventional blue-yellow complementary scheme. A profusion of the most differentiated yellows stands out against the midnight-blue background. A sonorously luminous blue responds at a few focal points. The numerous white flowers are sublimely shaded off with light brown, light gray, or light blue. The master employs only a very few red accents.

The bouquet is composed of a group of large flowers that is seen at a glance and a wealth of small blossoms among them, frequently intersecting, which cannot be taken in at a glance. They constitute the vibrating neutral background, as it were, against which each of the large flowers stands out by itself. In this lordly arrangement of the large flowers we see the sure architectonic touch of the master. They cross only at a few points. The naïve juxtaposition of the large flowers is an essential part of Bruegel's simplicity—simplicity stemming from a childlike, archaic way of seeing. That is why the story told by such a bouquet pleases one like a picture book. Only rarely do the strict architectonics of Jan's flower pieces seem affected (this is not true of his figurative paintings, such as those from the Allegory of the Five Senses series and the Paradise pictures), for flowers require a naïve and quiescent view.

Spring, summer, and autumn flowers bloom here side by side as a matter of course: snowdrops, daffodils, narcissus, grape hyacinths, cornflowers, pansies, buttercups, and bluebells from the fields; and the so-called most interesting flowers, roses, carnations, tulips, orange lilies, and irises from the cultivated garden. Considerable botanical insight is manifested in displaying the flowers from all sides: a rose is seen in profile; another is viewed from the underside, showing the long-fibered, recurved sepals; a tulip is fully open, so that its stigma and stamens can be easily "read." On the table a cyclamen, shown to botanical perfection with its blossoms, the top surface of its heart-shaped leaves, and the nodes and fibers on its roots, lives its own life.

Many insects animate the flowers. A mosquito walks over a rose on its six stiltlike legs; a butterfly clings to a rose-bud; a beetle craws across the table; and a tiger-striped caterpillar wriggles in an arched leaf. A grasshopper sways to and fro at the top left, and somewhat lower down there is a peacock butterfly with wings painted in great detail.

The curved, thickly haired borage stalks, the rustling, withered perianth of the narcissus, the golden-yellow anthers of the paper-white narcissus, and the dragonfly on the light-yellow tulip, with its rigid girdled body and its wing veins finer than a spider's web, hardly more than a breath of air despite the slight thickening of their ribbed edges (colorplate III), merit detailed study. The moist, wrinkled silkiness and ruffled contours of the irises that dominate the picture (colorplate IV) stand out, as do the fleshy, heavy, orange lily, the lush hyacinth, and the fragrant roses, floating as if suspended in space, which I call "Bruegel roses" because they reappear in all his flower still lifes (see colorplate VIII).

A still life within a still life, as it were, is depicted on the table. Jan's proud inquiry as to whether the flowers he painted did not "surpass gold and jewels" is put to the test here. The mineral materials, the coins and jewels, are a cool accent, setting off the warm, blooming flowers. The engraved coins and the translucent crystals create a noble world of their own. These precious objects, which are hidden beneath the bouquet as if subservient to it, imperceptibly elevate the plants themselves into the realm of jewelry.

Although the whole luminous composition of blossoms is wreathed in indistinct, warm-green leaves, and although a strong frontal light strikes the clay jar giving it plasticity, the entire flower piece does not convey a fully plastic effect. Bathed in a cool, silky light, the bouquet stands in imaginary space.

What is interesting, its splendor, is conspicuous, but the picture also contains something inscrutable. The fact that such exotic flowers as hyacinths, orange lilies, and Turk's-cap lilies grow out of a bouquet of field flowers conveys a singularly paradisiacal mood. Here we have the most precious gems blooming in a rural meadow of flowers.

Then there is the timeless juxtaposition of spring, summer, and autumn flowers, the brilliance of princely ornaments, and the strange, concealed life of all kinds of insects. They combine to weave a fairylike magic within the picture. No doubt the child in the painter saw a dream of Paradise here. It is that which gives the work its quiet magic. The picture is dominated by the age-old domestic flowers, rather than by the exotic ones; irises and roses constitute the fundamental chord. The bouquet is topped by three irises (colorplates II and IV), which is why I call it Bruegel's "Iris Bouquet." In the tradition of sacred paintings, the colored iris is the symbol of the Incarnate Son of God, while the white lily is the symbol of the Annunciation. The rose is Mary's symbol. This is another vestige of the age-old, mystical meaning of these flowers, for all the botanical precision with which they are reproduced.

Yet the dream of Paradise is merely the veiled, remote significance of the painting. What is obvious is botanical pride, and it is this to which the viewer initially responds. The first thing the layman asks about is the subject and the verifiable correctness of the rendering. The painter's actual accomplishment in intellectual conception, rhythmics, freedom, and penetration is more deeply hidden.

As we know, it is the skillful choice and treatment of the subject that spells failure or outward success in an artist's life, rather than his artistic achievement. Jan Bruegel was lucky in his choice of flowers as his subject, though he may hardly have had an inkling of his good luck. It was his botanical intelligence, in particular, that contributed to his lasting effect, rather than merely the conservative element in a gift of flowers as such (reduced today to the common-place of a flower-decorated telegram), or the generally colorful and decorative (which is also employed to decorate a box of chocolates), or the more profound, living, intrinsically joyous aspect of all blossoms.

This intelligence may be discerned at four points: in the extremely broad range of kinds and species of flowers known to the painter; in the microscopically accurate fineness of his observation (involucral spathes, variations in individual species, flower stalks, petioles); in the skill with which the plant's vegetative structure and respiratory

VII *Bouquet ("Lily Bouquet"). Detail of plate 4

systems are faithfully recorded; and in the profusion with which the same flowers are depicted in ever-new aspects, ever-new attitudes and postures.

Jan Bruegel usually painted his flowers directly from nature, without using drawings or oil sketches.[24] That is why we have hardly any flower sketches done by him, although we do have many sketches of landscapes and genre subjects. Sometimes he waited for a particularly costly flower to bloom (at least that is what he wrote in a letter to Cardinal Borromeo), and used that argument to pacify his impatient client. He traveled to Brussels frequently, to study and paint rare flowers in the Archduke's garden.

This sort of botanical work with a magnifying glass catered, of course, to the fashionable flower cult of the Renaissance and the Baroque. The pleasure derived from exotic show pieces attracted the spectator's botanical curiosity. The art of portrayal in many variations created true, virtually copybook, portraits of flowers.

No wonder that contemporary critics regarded him as a marvel: "Thus I propose to climb to the summit of art, which Jan Bruegel (who is called Flower Bruegel) has brought to light so well, giving me so much to write about that my pen seems to be too weak to describe his importance as a painter adequately, for he was not only an experienced painter of little figures and landscapes, which he did so excellently that nature itself could not have done better, but also because he was so excellent in flower painting that his refinement and sweet manner almost reproduced life itself."[25]

Jan Bruegel, who might literally be called a "painter of the magnifying glass," derived his microscopic grasp from the substantive, realistic Low Country way of seeing things, as well as from the particular tradition of miniature painting to which he was born. As a child he learned his craft from his grandmother, Mayken Verhulst, the miniaturist. No doubt Mayken began by teaching him how to do drawings and watercolors of figures and plants. From his early childhood he was able to draw upon a rich and differentiated storehouse of forms.

The artist gradually developed this serious and noble, painstaking vision and his academic knowledge of plants into a virtuosity "that is not to be found in other masters"[26] of flower painting.

The painter's strength as well as his limitations lay in this magnifying-glass exactitude. Seeing things from a miniaturist standpoint need not be an indication of pettiness. In the case of Jan Bruegel it is a sign of his contemplative dwelling on the subtle.[27] The pure, childlike joy that nourished Jan's pictures came from contemplation. Nor did he lack the ability to construct large compositions; he had a sure, constructive hand (which became even surer in the mature Jan, when we compare his late work with his early paintings). "Clarity is Bruegel's prime identification mark."[28]

With a sovereign touch Jan Bruegel assembled the wealth of detail, seen luminously and with a miniaturist's intensity, into his composition. He did not build dynamically like his father, but rather, like a Mannerist, singularly hard and almost severe at times. His composition, especially in the flower pieces, captivates us by its apparent "artlessness,"[29] which is the mark of virtuosity, yet his casual use of color is disciplined and always controlled. The obligatory color values remain within the confines of the conservative scheme of complements.

Cool colors of yellow and blue predominate in the "Iris Bouquet" (colorplate II), while the *Sheaf of Flowers in a Wooden Bucket* is dominated by the warmer polarity of red and green. The Vienna version of this "Crown Imperial Bouquet," as I call it, is shown in plate 3, while the larger Munich version is used as our frontispiece. A detail of this painting is shown in colorplate I. Here the red spreads over the whole picture in strong tones, from the glowing deep red of the carnations at the base of the bouquet to the rich light-red arc of tulips and orange lilies halfway up and the burning pinnacle of crown imperial, Turk's-cap lily, and peony at the top. Broad masses of green, shading into brown, balance out the power of the many reds.

VIII *Flowers.* Detail of plate 12

The warm fundamental tone is neutralized by many whites (purest in the huge stalk of Madonna lilies) and by the cool old rose of the Bruegel roses. The scattered blues, especially the irises and cornflowers, allow one's eye to rest.

This is the largest of the flower pieces, although Bruegel repeated this work seven or eight times in different sizes. The largest, nearly fifty inches high, is in Munich. It looks like a tower of flowers.

This flower piece differs from the more classic, more elegant "Iris Bouquet" in possessing a Baroque abundance, which makes it something joyous and a bit rustic.

As in the "Iris Bouquet," an orderly network of large flowers stretches over the web of innumerable finely studied little blossoms and berries. Thus the rustic idyl of snowdrops, forget-me-nots, buttercups, borage, squills, and white violets is held together by the two blood-red carnations at the rim of the bucket.

The entire colorfully flashing garden is dominated by a simple triad: Madonna lily, crown imperial, and peony.

The details display the wealth of the blossom-and-leaf fabric. The triple constellation of white lilies seems to capture all the light coming from the left. The crown imperial (colorplate I), which looks so exotic to a Western eye, with its leaves pointing upward like swords and its fiery flowers opening downward like an umbrella, is somewhat like the ancient mythical images of the sun. Enthroned against the dark background, it is the picture's focal point. The peony at the right, whose scarlet glows quietly among the restless play of light and shadow on the leaves, counterbalances the white lilies.

Interest in insects is traditional: a ladybug on the table down in front, another in the foliage; butterflies above the cyclamen at the left, on the mulberry branch at the right, and in the bouquet; and a fly on the fully opened white Bruegel rose, facing the viewer.

Here are a few other examples. The Berlin *Bouquet* (plate 4) is another quite typical flower piece, a surpassingly cultivated array of colors. (The repetitions of this painting resemble one another much less than in the case of the "Crown Imperial Bouquet.")

I should like to call the Berlin *Bouquet*, which culminates in a huge bunch of lilies, the "Lily Bouquet." A plethora of flowers is gathered in the lower part of the spray. Toward the top the bouquet spreads out in several large blossoms. The dominant color chord is orange-green. Broad white and old-rose areas harmonize and ennoble the chord. The detail (colorplate VII) exhibits the whole range of the Bruegel roses, whose bright atmospheric beauty manifests the transparent brush strokes of Jan Bruegel's training in watercolor.

The cluster of white Madonna lilies (colorplate VI) rises above the ripe orange of the tulips and fire lilies. The pure, sumptuous white is intensified by the surrounding blues of the iris. Lily and iris, ancient sacred symbols, provide a spiritually tranquil accent.

The painting's branch of currants at the right on the table is a finely poetic botanical study. Sunny, golden-green leaves alternate with brownish-black ones; leaf, stem, and veins are observed in the interplay of light and shadow from all sides, in all variations. The lower portion of the branch is almost a printing-ink black, while the upper part gleams in clear brightness. Glistening berries grow in panicles at varying distances; the upper part of the branch still has tender buds. A delicate dragonfly is balanced on the edge of a leaf. A hawk moth, with its patterned coat, antennae thickened at the front ends, and transparent, finely veined wings, has settled at the foot of the vase at the left.

The elegant vase, decorated with reliefs and medallions, the strikingly rich whites, and the crown of lilies and irises—all combine to give this work its serious, somewhat stiff appearance.

The "Tulip Bouquet" (plate 2) is much brighter and gayer. The center is built up on a childlike pure red, which is mirrored in a cool violet at the top and in a light old rose at the bottom. The unusually large bearded iris (colorplate V) is a reticent, dark, grayish blue. This bouquet contains less white than any other of Jan Bruegel's paintings. It also branches out more than any other; the bouquet seems to be shooting out in all directions. The little flowers that

IX PETER PAUL RUBENS and JAN BRUEGEL THE ELDER. *Madonna in a Wreath of Flowers*. Panel, $72^7/_8 \times 82^5/_8''$

surround it loosen the conventional tightness of the composition. In this picture the artist also attempted several original overlappings of blossoms. The "Tulip Bouquet" is doubtless the freest, gayest, and most dynamic of his flower pieces.

The *Vase of Flowers* (plate 5), a late painting, exhibits an impressively silent concentration. There are hardly any embellishments to distract the eye. A few bright points of emphasis fill the free space. This is a painting of tender pathos. The fine, long filaments of the fairy flax's starry white blossoms at the left of the picture are reproduced with botanical accuracy.

The two other small works of his late period, the *Bowl of Flowers* (plate 6) and *Flowers on a Dish* (plate 7), exhale a fragrant, poetic charm.

Another late work, the *Still Life with Garland of Flowers* (plate 8), ventures a more intellectual language, endeavoring to combine the warmth of vegetation with subtle, costly, cool jewelry. There is a charming sketch for this composition (page 29).

At this point we should discuss Jan's collaborative work.

Jan Bruegel decorated several works by other artists with flowers or figures. Artistic collaboration along these lines is an age-old phenomenon, of course. It is based on the notion of great inspiration, say, in the Pentecostal sense. (Icon painting has continued this tradition into modern times.)

The service of a common vision was the force that supported the medieval masons' "lodges"; that is why unanimity was the supreme injunction of all the early artisans' confraternities. The urban guilds, such as the painters' Guild of St. Luke founded in Antwerp in 1382, grew out of the masons' lodges. Other crafts also united to form corporations of this kind, which looked after their members' interests: carpet weavers, goldsmiths, and trades related to painting, such as picture dealers, glass painters, etc. As the years went by, an ever-increasing trend toward specialization developed out of these workshops.

The guilds defended their statutes less strictly than in the Middle Ages, to be sure (women, for example, were allowed to paint, rather than merely to grind colors as before), but artists traveling to study still enjoyed the hospitality of their fellows in foreign countries, for the customs of the Guilds of St. Luke prevailed in one form or another through all the countries of Western Europe. An artist did not pursue his art chiefly as a means of earning a living; being an artist was a noble way of life, which involved obligations and conferred rights.

Evidently Jan Bruegel was well adapted to the craft-guild mode of thought. He acted as master of a company, and for two years he headed the Antwerp guild.

The collaboration of Quentin Massys and Joos van Cleve with Joachim Patinir is probably one of the oldest instances of teamwork by Low Country painters in easel pictures that has come down to us. In the seventeenth century, when the art of Flanders was in its prime, collaboration, which was especially popular there, developed to such an extent that it was not uncommon for five different artists to work on a single painting. One did the figures, another did the interiors, a third did the landscapes, a fourth did the architecture, and a fifth did the incidental decorative objects.[30] Jan Bruegel worked together with many colleagues, above all Rubens, for whom he painted backgrounds when the scale was small enough, but also vistas, flowers, fruits, faces, etc. Documents and joint signatures prove that he did this not as a subordinate assistant, but as an equal. On the other hand, the German Hans Rottenhammer and Pieter van Avont (see plate 9) added figures to Bruegel's landscapes and religious pictures, while Hendrick van Balen and Henri de Clerck chiefly painted the human figures for his allegories and mythological paintings. Nor did Rubens regard this occasional favor below his dignity. Bruegel painted in the figures in Joos de Mompers' pictures and did the same on occasion for Van Balen, and Van Balen sometimes did so for Bruegel. Other contemporaries

X *The Village Street.* Copper, $7^1/_8 \times 10''$

with whom Jan collaborated were Paul Bril, Frans Francken II, Pieter Neefs the Younger, and Sebastiaen Vrancx (plate 18).

Inner affinity, the same spiritual bond shared by the artists, is a prerequisite for artistic collaboration. But when we examine the paintings that Jan Bruegel created with his partners, this spiritual accord is seldom to be found. On the contrary, their individualities are manifested with a Renaissance-like independence. The component parts do not fuse together in these works. A surprisingly clear structure is produced, owing to the very different styles that clash here, but the double nature of the experiment is evident in these works.

Here are two examples.

Pieter van Avont, thirty-one years younger than Bruegel, painted *The Holy Family*, and Jan did the garland for it (plate 9). Pieter van Avont's picture tells a pleasant story, but it is the work of Jan Bruegel that gives the picture its jewel-like magic.

This garland, which suggests the sacred monogram MARIA in its *porta triumphalis*, is charming, as if constructed in childlike merriment. A kind of maternal, earthy fertility is set forth with broad rusticity in roots and herbs, fruits and seeds, leaves and flowers.

The sacrificial magic of antiquity, rural harvest customs, and a fairylike dream of Paradise are blended together in the garland. Culinary delights seem to have been in the forefront of the painter's fancy, yet the wealth of bloom and fruit is merely a ritual. Earthly beauty is merged into the otherwordly enchantment of the "enclosed garden."

Noah's ark, another instance of Biblical grace, is suggested by the peaceable round of animals, often ordered in pairs. His method is amusing: the sketch shows part of the garland; the painting has a bird wherever there is a space in the sketch.

The decorative ornamentation is far superior artistically to the amicable unproblematical work, though a certain fundamental mood of contemplative meditation pervades the whole.

This is not the case in Jan Bruegel's collaboration with Rubens, who was nine years his junior. Here both painters operate at the same high level. On the other hand, the intrinsic key, the interior style, is not harmonious. One instance is the celebrated *Madonna in a Wreath of Flowers* in Munich (colorplate IX). This is the largest of the paintings discussed here; the wreath alone is fifty-nine inches in diameter.

Bruegel's wreath reminds one of the Baroque rhythms of the "Crown Imperial Bouquet." If we try to separate the flower painting visually from the painting as a whole, viewing it by itself, we begin to realize the power of the composition and its own tranquil light. The organically irregular wreath, which broadens out at the base of the painting, has its center of gravity at the very bottom, in the red of the peonies.

Flowers playfully echo the red of the Madonna's robe all around the wreath. The blue of her cloak is repeated in lighter variations; the Bruegel roses set off Rubens' opalescent flesh tints with their cooler, more austere old rose. The devotion of Jan's work is manifested in this faithful harmony with the portrait of the Madonna.

Rubens' tempo was alien to Bruegel's circumspection. The wreath is like a timeless island alongside the virtuosity of the lines and the brilliant play of light in Rubens' work. Rubens tried to weave the flower painting into the picture more elegantly in several places. The intersecting branches and the hollyhock blossoms in the wings of the angel at the right are his work. His more practiced line is recognizable at a glance.

Yet the quietly blossoming wreath constitutes a monastically pious, self-contained world in the whole vibrant work. The merely accessory, "gentle" flowers embody much more religion than the accomplished sensuality of the religious nudes.

XI   *The Road to Market.* Copper, $7^1/_4 \times 10''$

It is not by chance that the lilies and iris bloom close to the Christ Child's head, while the fragrant roses are placed below the Madonna as if in prayer. The strongest red in the picture, the red of the peonies, glows at the bottom of the sacred picture as a symbol of glorification.

Still another theme belongs in this chapter: the Allegory of the Five Senses. In cold fact, this theme is interesting chiefly in connection with the history of ideas; its significance as an artistic phenomenon does not extend beyond a certain period.

This theme, which appears around 1500 (as in a series of Walloon tapestries), was related to Scholastic and Humanist ideas. The allegory, a personification of an abstract concept that is rarely successful, was a surviving vestige of Scholasticism. The peculiar meditative content of the five senses is understandable as part of the comprehensive process of rethinking that was one of the motive forces of the Renaissance. Deductive thought, evolving from the mind, was slowly, step by step, replaced by object-oriented induction.

The senses were rethought and ennobled as servants of the mind.

This process of rethinking—from Leonardo da Vinci, who was the first to speak of the decisive importance of experiment, through the Spanish Humanist Juan Luis Vives[31] and Galileo, who founded consistently scientific thought, to Francis Bacon, who developed the inductive method most clearly—this rethinking, aided by an extensive didactic literature, spread to many walks of life.

Inductive thinking—not to be confused with uncritically accumulating, purely empirical thought—elaborates its judgments on the basis of sensory experiences, which have to be critically sifted, however, like "vintage," as Bacon puts it. Reflection was thus assigned a wholly new key position in intellectual life.

The new orientation was popularly understood as the involvement of intelligence with material existence.

This meaningful watchword, which liberated man from the hierarchical manner of thinking of the Middle Ages, was then seized upon by the populace and applied in a wide variety of connections, as in the subject of the Allegory of the Five Senses in painting.

After the theme had been adopted and developed as a purely graphic subject in the sixteenth century (Frans Floris is supposed to have been the pioneer, about 1500), Jan Bruegel was the first to transpose the subject into a painting (1617).

Jan's allegories of the senses (plates 10–12) are laden with all the complicated apparatus of allegorical subject matter, most of which was discarded later in the seventeenth century. These pictures suffer appreciably under the burden of what is still a semimedieval miscellany. Their real attractiveness lies in their details, where the master's pleasure in flowers unconcernedly persists. In the painting shown in plate 12, Bruegel's entire wealth of flowers blooms in front of a delightful park landscape that is somewhat stiff in composition. Behind the flowers there is an old-fashioned perfume still with delicate flasks and retorts. The charming rose-picking scene in the background seems to allude to the fact that the dying flower is transmuted into aromatic essences, while in the foreground we have a wealth of freshly cut, "sacrificed" roses, brushed in more freely than in all his other pictures (colorplate VIII).

Other animals have joined the merry insect population in the flowers in the foreground. An unusually small chipmunk stares wide-eyed at the flood of roses. A colorful parrot watches mistrustfully over the carnations, which are supported by stakes. The cock of the peafowl pair bows in the middle of the picture, his tail iridescent with all the colors of the rainbow and ornamented with brightly colored eyes. Four does, symbols of gentleness and peace, do

XII *Travelers in a Landscape*. Detail of plate 19

not permit their tranquillity to be disturbed by human proximity and industry. Quite to the contrary, the recumbent doe is looking attentively at the evidence of this activity: the little furnace with its blazing red fire, the retorts, the stills, and the other vessels.

The telescope, which enables the eye to penetrate distance, must be present in *Sight* (plate 10). Rather more important, however, is the magnifying glass, the key to the world of the minute. The macrocosmos (represented by the globe in the background) and the microcosmos (represented by the precious objects on the table) both belong to the world of the eye, a cosmos in the sense of the "eternal ornament."

Stürmische See   Stormy Sea   Ehemalige Staatliche Museen, Berlin, Kupfer[

Waldweg   A Woodland Road   British Museum, London

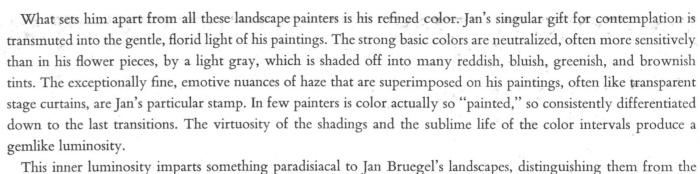

Hafenszene Harbour Scene British Museum, London

What sets him apart from all these landscape painters is his refined color. Jan's singular gift for contemplation is transmuted into the gentle, florid light of his paintings. The strong basic colors are neutralized, often more sensitively than in his flower pieces, by a light gray, which is shaded off into many reddish, bluish, greenish, and brownish tints. The exceptionally fine, emotive nuances of haze that are superimposed on his paintings, often like transparent stage curtains, are Jan's particular stamp. In few painters is color actually so "painted," so consistently differentiated down to the last transitions. The virtuosity of the shadings and the sublime life of the color intervals produce a gemlike luminosity.

This inner luminosity imparts something paradisiacal to Jan Bruegel's landscapes, distinguishing them from the ceremonial, ideal landscapes of the Bril and Elsheimer circle.

The fundamental tectonic laws of a landscape picture established by Pieter Bruegel the Elder were richly varied by Van Coninxloo and Bril, but they retained their validity. The entire landscape space is something like a stage-setting landscape, notwithstanding its more fluent, freer rhythm and the deepening of the center of light, which unfolds as the "soul" of the picture. The foreground and the middle distance slide in front of the elevated distant view (which usually terminates quietly), often producing a silhouette effect. The perspective is usually chosen from an ideal, slightly elevated standpoint. The paintings appear to be considerably denser than the loose drawings, which produce a much more "modern" effect.

Thus the poetic, the almost literary element is a controlling factor in Jan Bruegel's landscapes (plates 13–15 and colorplates X–XVI).

The composition of *The Village Street*[33] (colorplate X), a well-balanced little picture in silvery, cool colors, is very simple, like a child's story. A deliberately foreshortened road that fills nearly the entire width of the painting leads into the picture, as in several other works bearing the same title. Two horsemen, one of them in profile and the other seen from the rear, fill in the foreground so commandingly as to draw one's eyes into the picture. The lyrically dreamy pond, the tall inn, drawn in a velvety greenish brown, the leisurely groups of people, animals, and carts compose the middle distance in an apparently fortuitous arrangement. The sails of a windmill rotate up on the hill, imparting the mood of an untroubled, contemplative peace to the painting. A covered wagon is barely visible in the pale-gold distance. A church, houses, and trees compose a distant vision bathed in sunlight.

The harmonious blend of colors in the picture, flowing together in an infinitely modified gray, and multifariously modulated red, blue, green, and brown, coincides with the balanced tectonics, as in the flower pieces. Gray shades off into reddish, bluish, greenish, and brownish tints, like the white in a bouquet, so that the road, colored a gentle grayish blue, is most subtly differentiated from the slate-blue hill, the brownish-green clumps of trees, and the pinkish-brown row of buildings. A pale-blue sky, shading off into white gold at the left (against which the pink corbiestep gable stands out squarely), transfigures the ensemble of colors. Most carefully graduated veils of haze bring even the most colorful counterpoints (such as the bright-red blouse and luminous-blue skirt of the woman chatting with the horseman) into equilibrium, elevating this everyday scene into something atmospheric.

When we examine Jan's brush strokes, we come to understand the many-layered poetry of his narrative. Another idyl called *Village Street* (plate 13), a tiny work, smaller than a postcard, which we reproduce somewhat enlarged, also exhibits the velvety density and art of this texture. This picture is once again divided into clear surfaces by the simplest perspective. The procession of figures ends in an uncommonly hazy distance. Fine-spun branches play around the peaceful cubes of the houses. A golden sky shines over the picture. It may be the fine concentration that gives the original its magic.

The painting *River Scene with Boats and Figures* (plate 15 and colorplate XIV) contains an abundance of such poetic scenes. It is a sequence of details exhibiting different rhythms and color moods. The left background, a delightful

XIII *Market and Outdoor Laundry in Flanders*. Canvas, $65^3/_8 \times 76^3/_8''$

The *Stormy Sea* (page 51) is Jan's most beautiful sketch. The storm is drawn in splendidly fresh, rapid pen-and-ink strokes, with waves, sails, robes, and movements. The brush washes in a few brown and blue tints.

The little work *Jonah's Deliverance from the Whale* (plate 16), hardly eighteen inches high, is truly luscious. The heroic mountain landscape is evidence that this is an early work. The agitated events extend from the sky, black as night and countered by the light at the right, to the steep, craggy coastline and the luminously colorful sea. And yet Jan has employed his magic to introduce his lyricism into the picture covertly: the bay rests peacefully in the background; the fairy castle gleams among the rocks; shellfish and snails glitter on the shore; and a story-book whale looks upward piously.

The even earlier *Burning of Troy* (plate 17) conceals a similar magic. The reddish-orange fire is not merely terrifying, it is also festive, lighting up a fantastic golden city. Despite all their dramatic quality, the fleeing figures in the foreground are full of poetry. The brilliantly lighted scene has four areas of light: in the foreground the glittering group of people; behind them the brightly illuminated, wild turmoil around the Trojan Horse; the moon up above; and at the center of the picture a threefold gradation—flaming lights, gleaming water, and the boat's lantern.

The turbulent figures in the landscape of *The Ambush* (plate 18) are by Sebastiaen Vrancx, rather than Bruegel. Jan has enveloped the grisly slaughter in a pleasing, forested frame. Even the gallows in the background has something graceful and amusing about it.

Whenever Jan's landscapes exceed a certain "gem" format in size, they lose something of their power. The details are always brilliant and full of charm, but the expansive, monumental rhythm is missing.

Jan's large landscapes therefore often appear to be short-winded and vague. They often look like touching mosaics constructed of beautiful, glowing little pieces. The master is unable to fuse the mosaic together with a single vital stroke.

An instance of this is the large painting, *Harbor with Christ Preaching*. Christ preaching in a boat, the central event of the picture, is hard to find, even in the colorful original (colorplate XV). The picture is a colossal miniature, an encyclopedic world theater. One's eye wants to wander over the cosmic landscape rising at the horizon, but it is caught in the confusion of the countless puppet figures that burst apart the foreground.

Concluding this chapter, let us mention two forest landscapes, one of which, *Forest Road by a Riverbank*, is reproduced here (plate 20). Both of them are again in the small format in which Jan felt at home. Here Bruegel is obviously influenced by Van Coninxloo, though his rendering is more realistic, a bit harder. The *Forest Road* boldly and astonishingly juxtaposes two halves, one dark and the other light. The picture is united into a whole by the counter-movement as well as the striking parallel movement in both halves.

Rest on the Flight, the other forest landscape, has a single big tree, really a double tree, at its center. The interpenetration and counteraction of the young tree and the old are highly musical. Light strikes the old tree from the dark, forest side, while the young tree rises darkly at the edge of the clearing.

The theme compels the master to use figures sparingly; the poetic, tiny figures thus appear to be larger, constituting the bright, joyous center, in contrast to the oppressive darkness of the woods. The British Museum, London, has an impressive sketch for this painting (page 49).

XV *Harbor with Christ Preaching.* Panel, 30³/₄ × 46⁷/₈″

XVI *Entering the Ark.* Copper, $10^1/_8 \times 14^5/_8$

Paradise Bruegel

The art of Jan Bruegel the Elder is epitomized in his Paradise landscapes.

It is true that nearly everything Jan painted is part of a single "fairy garden," a paradise, as it were. But it is only a part, and we can only infer the religious background of which it is a part. But the Paradise pictures combine Jan's flower painting and Jan's landscapes into a higher, meaningful unity.

Jan, "Flower Bruegel," is also called by another, less common nickname, "Paradise Bruegel." This name may refer to the paradisiacal charm of his colors and his brush strokes. At the same time it suggests Bruegel's way of seeing things, like a sleepwalker, seeing "une image de paradis"[34] in all things—the childlike faith that the true Paradise exists somewhere in space or time.

An artist who is always "on the road to paradise" in his painting comes home, as it were, in the Paradise genre. Paradise completes the idyl.

Every age, every philosophy, every ideology constructs its own variation of this primordial myth: from Judaism's Garden of Eden to the utopias of the idealist philosophers, from the Greek Olympus to the Communist utopia of Karl Marx, from the Paradise of the old Persian myth (the word is Avestan in origin) to Schelling's Church of the Spirit, from the crystalline "Heavenly Jerusalem" of the Apocalypse to the "new religion" sought by Franz Marc, and to the future "great spiritual epoch" of which Wassily Kandinsky dreamed.

Broad as the range of these variations is, the essential features are ever-recurrent: freedom, peace, refuge, everlasting life, and spiritual rebirth.

The painter's eye sees all of these things pictorially. Freedom is conveyed by growth and movement. Peace is conveyed by the untroubled coexistence of plants, animals, and man. Refuge is expressed in the hedge-like, overhanging trees. Everlasting life is conveyed by the simultaneous blooming of all flowers, and rebirth by the diffuse, otherworldly light (which also pervades Jan's flower pieces and landscapes).

We shall confine our attention to a few examples.

Is *Paradise* (plate 23), where the two principal figures were painted by Rubens, a successful experiment? The tree of knowledge is cut off at the top of the picture; the horizon is so low that the ostrich's neck and the "principal actors" project far above it, in contrast to the usual Bruegel figures, which are positioned below the horizon. The Fall of Man takes place in bright sunlight, at the very footlights, so to speak. The marvelously beautiful serpent—the archetype of cunning that evades all traps—coils around a branch in the shadow.

The earth, painted a light ocher throughout, and the transparent, verdigris-colored water exhibit numerous perfect animal portraits, done in many shades of brown and gray. Above there is a cobalt-blue sky with white, midsummer clouds.

The painting, crammed with details and suffering from several inconsistencies of composition, achieves a certain unity only by the discipline with which Jan handled color. The two basic colors of the picture, warm green and warm brown, are unusually well modulated and shaded down to the last detail. Red occurs only in a few accents: the forbidden apples, the parrots, and the tigers' mouths. The painter is even more sparing of blue (the peacock). To make up for this, he developed a vigorous scale of whites: from a cold, steel white (the swans and pigs), through chalk white (the Maltese dog and the rabbit) and silver (the turkey cock), to a warm, golden white (the fallow deer and midsummer clouds). With this highly cultivated use of color, Bruegel did manage to forge the painting into an astonishing whole.

The Berlin *Paradise* (colorplates XVII and XVIII) is an energetic composition of classic clarity. The three intertwined trees—the first one providing a splendid diagonal support to the composition, the second one spreading over the whole picture, and the vertically supporting third tree—set up a powerful structure, which is continued in the little plants in the foreground. The animals, fewer in number than in the other Paradise pictures, are organically woven into the rhythm of the forest.

The more subtly designed Frankfort *Garden of Eden* (plate 22) includes the creation of Eve from the rib of the sleeping Adam. This truly exciting scene, painted in a healthy, matter-of-fact manner, takes place in a sacred botanical and zoological garden.

The Earthly Paradise in Paris (plate 21) follows a related compositional plan. The creatures are distributed with regard to the clear structuring of the whole (as is always the case with Bruegel) in encyclopedic abundance, though not always highly organically. The subjects, each in a different scale, stand alongside one another, more or less at random; this is more noticeable than in Bruegel's true-to-life landscapes. God the Father, cloaked in a long, flowing robe, is no larger than the tulip blossom seen in the right foreground. Jan Bruegel "painted" down to the last detail even the darkest parts of the picture, which most of the painters of the time (such as Adriaen Brouwer and David Teniers the Younger) simply skimmed over. This "review" of the most intimate nature brings out the warmth of the painting, which is more like brocade than velvet.

Entering the Ark (colorplate XVI), a paradisiacal subject in the wider sense of the term, is probably the most mature of Jan's Paradise pictures. The tectonic form is cool and sure: the leafless tree in the foreground, actually nothing but a trunk with a few limbs, barely intersects the horizon at the center; the wide clearing in the valley is repeated on a narrower scale; while the two vertical clusters of trees balance and support the composition. The creek and the column of animals end quietly and inevitably in the ark. The tension of the event transforms the paradisiacal peace into a dynamic happening. The menacing sky at the right, in which the colorful birds still sparkle, gives way to the heavy, cobalt-blue cloud banks, which herald the impending flood. Flocks of birds hover in the air. The animal column, slowly getting under way, gives the playful confusion of animals an orientation and meaning. The ark itself, which is schematically hidden in the background above the family of Noah, is almost as hard to find as if this were a picture puzzle. The drama of the story is reflected in the colors. Black, blue, green, and ocher predominate, with a few red accents in between. The dark light in which the action takes place gives it seriousness and inwardness.

The Inquisition's shadow of death, which also grazed this later painter of the sunny side of life, had vanished, and it seemed as if it had been sublimated into the "golden cheerfulness" that smiles at the beholder in these works, though we should remember that these pictures were produced under living conditions that must appear to us today as primitive, even miserable. But now as then Jan Bruegel's pastoral landscapes, pictures of Paradise, and never-fading flower bouquets are the joy of the art-loving world.

I PETER PAUL RUBENS The Family of Jan Bruegel 1612–13 Panel, 49 x 37 1/2″

2 Bouquet
in a Blue Vase
(*Tulpenstrauss*)
Panel, 26 x 20″

Large Bouquet in
Wooden Tub
(*Kaiserkronenstrauss*)
anel, 37³/₄ x 28³/₄"

4   Bouquet *(Lilienstrauss)*   Panel, 25 1/4 x 23 1/4"

5   Vase of Flowers *(Blumenglas)*   Panel, 18¹/₂ x 13³/₄″

6   Bowl of Flowers *(Kleiner Rosenteller)*   Canvas, 17 x 13″

7 Flowers on a Dish
   (Rosenschale)
   Panel, $17^{1}/_{4}$ x 26″

8 Still Life with Garland of Flowers 1618
   Panel, $18^{3}/_{4}$ x $20^{1}/_{2}$″

9 JAN BRUEGEL and PIETER VAN AVONT ▷
   The Holy Family Panel, $36^{3}/_{4}$ x $28^{1}/_{4}$″

10 Sight, from *The Five Senses*   Canvas, 76³/₄ x 103¹/₂″

11 Taste, from *The Five Senses*   1618   Panel, 25¹/₄ x 42¹/₂″

12 Touch, from *The Five Senses*   Panel, 25¹/₂ x 43″

13 Village Street 1610 Copper, 3 1/4 x 5"

Detail

4 Outskirts of a Village 1597
Copper, 11¼ x 14½″

Detail

15 River Scene with Boats and Figures 1606 Copper, 11 1/4 x 16 3/4"

16 Jonah's Deliverance from the Whale Panel, 15 x 22"

17 The Burning of Troy Copper, 10 1/4 x 14"

18 JAN BRUEGEL and SEBASTIAEN VRANCX The Ambush Panel, 22 x 33$\frac{1}{2}$″

19 Travelers in a Landscape 1616 Copper, 10 x 14$\frac{1}{2}$″

20   Forest Road by a Riverbank   Copper, 13 x 18³/₄"

21   The Earthly Paradise (*Earth*, from *The Four Elements*)   Copper, 18 x 26¹/₂"

22   The Garden of Eden (showing the Creation of Eve)   Copper, $11\frac{1}{2}$ x 15″

23   PETER PAUL RUBENS and JAN BRUEGEL   Paradise (Adam and Eve in the Garden)   Panel, 29 x 45″

Notes

1. We use the spelling Bruegel, both for Jan the Elder and for the other members of this family of painters. Jan Bruegel was not consistent himself in his signatures.

2. Cardinal Federigo Borromeo, Archbishop of Milan, was the nephew and successor of St. Charles Borromeo. Born in 1564, he died in 1631.

3. Jan Bruegel's letter to Cardinal Borromeo, dated July 8, 1605: in Guhl-Rosenberg, *Künstlerbriefe*, 2nd ed., Berlin, 1880. See note 2.

4. *Ibid.*, dated August 25, 1606.

5. Heinrich Wölfflin, *Das Erklären von Kunstwerken*, Cologne, 1940.

6. After Lottlisa Behling, *Die Pflanzenwelt der mittelalterlichen Kathedralen*, Cologne-Graz, 1964.

7. *Ibid.*

8. Liselotte Hansmann and Lenz Kriss-Rettenbeck, *Amulett und Talisman*, Munich, 1966.

9. After Irmgard Hampp, *Beschwörung Segen Gebet*, Stuttgart, 1961.

10. Behling, *op. cit.*

11. Fritz Burger, "Die deutsche Malerei vom ausgehenden Mittelalter bis zum Ende der Renaissance," *Handbuch der Kunstwissenschaft*, Vol. I, Berlin, 1913.

12. Germain Bazin, *Gallery of Flowers*, New York, 1964.

13. John Gerard, *Herball or Generall Historie of Plantes*, 1597 (?).

14. Yvonne Thiéry, *Le Paysage flamand au XVIIᵉ siècle*, Paris-Brussels, 1953.

15. *Ibid.*

16. Jean Baptiste Descamps, *La Vie des peintres flamands, allemands et hollandois*, Paris, 1753–64. ("His paintings were regarded as marvels, which spread his fame far and wide.")

17. See notes 2 and 3.

18. Jan Bruegel's letter to Cardinal Borromeo, dated 1606, *op. cit.*

19. Thiéry, *op. cit.*

20. Jacques Lassaigne and Robert Delevoy, *Flemish Painting*, Vol. II: *From Bosch to Rubens*, Cleveland, 1958.

21. Matthias Winner, "Zeichnungen des älteren Jan Brueghel," *Jahrbuch der Berliner Museen*, Vol. III, 1961.

22. Van Mander's statement that Jan's brother, Pieter the Younger, had also been a pupil of Gillis is probably a case of mistaken identity, according to Gerson (see Bibliography).

23. See note 2.

24. "Senza desseigni o boitssaturo" ("without designs or sketches"), as Jan wrote to Bianchi in his broken Italian in 1611.

25. Cornelis de Bie, *Het gulden Cabinet vande edel vry schilderconst*, Lier, 1661.

26. Marie-Louise Hairs, *Les Peintres flamands de fleurs au XVIIᵉ siècle*, Paris-Brussels, 1965.

27. Yvonne Thiéry, *op. cit.*: "Une contemplation attentive à la nuance la plus subtile" ("A contemplation attentive to the subtlest nuance").

28. Winner, *op. cit.*

29. Hairs, *op. cit.*

30. After A.J. Wauters, *La Peinture flamande*, Paris, 1883.

31. Juan Luis Vives, *De Anima et vita*, 1555.

32. Lassaigne and Delevoy, *op. cit.*

33. Other variants in the Landesmuseum, Hanover (*In Front of the Village Inn*, copper, $8^5/_8 \times 11^3/_8$", dated 1591), and in the Galerie Liechtenstein, Vaduz (slightly larger, dated 1597).

34. Jacques Combe, *Breughel de Velours*, Paris, 1942.

Chronological outline

This chronological table endeavors to relate the lives of the Bruegel family members to the events of their time. Primary emphasis has been given to events that are related to the history of the Low Countries and to the world of art. Entries closely related to Jan Bruegel the Elder are set in italics. Jan stands for Jan Bruegel the Elder.

1502	Erasmus of Rotterdam: "Handbook of the Militant Christian." *Pieter Coecke van Aelst, painter and scholar, Jan's grandfather, born in Aelst*
1503–8	Gerard David: "The Baptism of Christ"
1505–10	Tilman Riemenschneider: "The Creglingen Altarpiece"
1512–16	Grünewald (Mathis Gothart Nithardt): Isenheim Altar
1516	Hieronymus Bosch dies in 's Hertogenbosch
1517	Martin Luther: "The Ninety-five Theses"
c. 1520	*Marie Bessemers (Mayken Verhulst), miniaturist, Jan's grandmother, born in Mechlin*
1520	Martin Luther: "The Freedom of a Christian Man"
1520–21	Albrecht Dürer's journey through the Netherlands
c. 1525	*Pieter Bruegel the Elder ("Peasant Bruegel"), Jan's father, born in Breda*
1526	Lucas van Leyden: "Last Judgment Altarpiece" in Leyden
1529	Albrecht Altdorfer: "The Battle of Alexander"
c. 1530	Orlando di Lasso born
1550	*Pieter Coecke van Aelst dies in Brussels*
1564	*Pieter Bruegel the Younger ("Hell Bruegel"), Jan's elder brother, born in Brussels*
1568	*Jan Bruegel the Elder born in Brussels*
Sept. 5, 1569	*Pieter Bruegel the Elder dies in Brussels*
Aug. 24, 1572	Massacre of St. Bartholomew ("Parisian Massacre"): twenty thousand Huguenots murdered at the order of Catherine de Médicis
1572–85	Reign of Pope Gregory XIII, promoter of the Counter Reformation, patron of the Society of Jesus
1575–80	*Jan is taught the art of watercolor by his grandmother, Mayken Verhulst*
Aug. 27, 1576	Titian dies in Venice
June 28, 1577	Peter Paul Rubens born in Siegen, Westphalia
1577	Aggravated Counter Reformation in the Hapsburg possessions
1578–84	*Jan attends school in Antwerp and is taught painting by Pieter Goetkind and presumably by Gillis van Coninxloo as well*
1579	Union of the northern provinces proclaimed at Utrecht
1580–88	Montaigne: "Essays"
1581	The northern provinces break with Spain
1574–91	Giordano Bruno: philosophical writings
1587	Mary Queen of Scots executed
1588	Defeat of the Spanish Armada; end of Spain's dominion of the seas. Galileo discovers the law of oscillatory motion
c. 1589	*Jan travels to Italy via Cologne*
1590	*Jan in Naples*
1593–94	*Jan in Rome. He becomes acquainted with Cardinal Borromeo and enters his service in 1595*
1594	Shakespeare: "A Midsummer Night's Dream"
1596	*Jan works in Milan for Cardinal Borromeo*
1597	*After briefly traveling through Flanders and Holland, Jan settles in Antwerp. He becomes a Master of the Guild of St. Luke in Antwerp*
1598	Henry IV, King of France, issues the Edict of Nantes, granting the Huguenots some measure of religious freedom
1599	*Jan marries Isabella Jode, daughter of a copperplate engraver.* Van Dyck born in Antwerp
April, 1600	*Marie Bessemers (Mayken Verhulst) dies in Brussels*
1601	*Jan becomes a citizen of the city of Antwerp. Jan Bruegel the Younger born in Antwerp*

1601–2	Jan serves as Dean of the Guild of St. Luke in Antwerp
1603	Isabella, Jan's first wife, dies. Shakespeare: "Hamlet"
1605	Jan marries Catharina van Marienberghe
1605–15	Cervantes: "Don Quixote"
July 15, 1606	Rembrandt born in Leyden
1607	Monteverdi: "Orfeo"
1609	Archduke Albert and Archduchess Isabella appoint Jan court painter and grant him many privileges. Founding of the Catholic League in Germany
1610	Galileo discovers the moons of Jupiter
1610–20	Jan travels through Germany and Bohemia (Prague, Nuremberg, Heidelberg, Frankenthal)
1612–14	Rubens: "Descent from the Cross" in Antwerp
1614	El Greco dies
1615–20	Elias Holl: Town Hall, Augsburg
1618	The Defenestration of Prague. Beginning of the Thirty Years' War
1619	Jan owns five houses. Johannes Kepler: "Harmonice mundi"
Jan. 12, 1625	Jan dies of cholera in Antwerp
1627	Catharina van Marienberghe dies
May 30, 1640	Rubens dies in Antwerp

The Bruegel Family of Painters

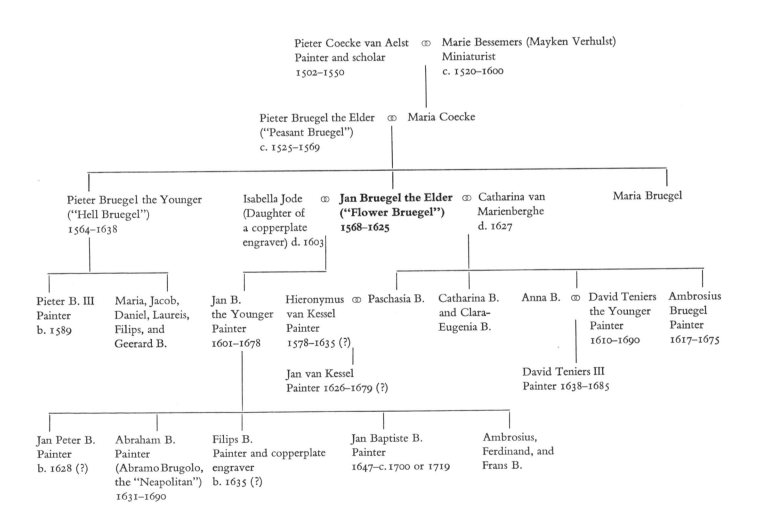

83

List of Colorplates

List of Black-and-White Illustrations

1 PETER PAUL RUBENS. *The Family of Jan Bruegel*, 1612–13. Panel, 49 × 37^1/$_2$″. Collection of Count Antoine Seilern, London

2 JAN BRUEGEL THE ELDER. *Bouquet in a Blue Vase ("Tulip Bouquet")*. Panel, 26 × 20″. Kunsthistorisches Museum, Vienna

3 JAN BRUEGEL THE ELDER. *Large Bouquet in a Wooden Tub ("Crown Imperial Bouquet")*. Panel, 37^3/$_4$ × 28^3/$_4$″. Kunsthistorisches Museum, Vienna. (Cf. the Munich version of the bouquet—Frontispiece)

4 JAN BRUEGEL THE ELDER. *Bouquet ("Lily Bouquet")*. Panel, 25^1/$_4$ × 23^1/$_4$″. State Museums, Berlin-Dahlem

5 JAN BRUEGEL THE ELDER. *Vase of Flowers ("Glass with Flowers")*. Panel, 18^1/$_2$ × 13^3/$_4$″. Ashmolean Museum, Oxford

6 JAN BRUEGEL THE ELDER. *Bowl of Flowers ("Small Rose Bowl")*. Canvas, 17 × 13″. Prado, Madrid

7 JAN BREUGEL THE ELDER. *Flowers on a Dish ("Rose Bowl")*. Panel, 17^1/$_4$ × 26″. Prado, Madrid

8 JAN BRUEGEL THE ELDER. *Still Life with Garland of Flowers*. Signed on the knife: "Brueghel fecit 1618." Panel, 18^3/$_4$ × 20^1/$_2$″. Musée Royale des Beaux Arts, Brussels

9 JAN BRUEGEL THE ELDER and PIETER VAN AVONT. *The Holy Family*. Panel, 36^3/$_4$ × 28^1/$_4$″. Alte Pinakothek, Munich

10 JAN BRUEGEL THE ELDER. *Sight* from "The Five Senses." Canvas, 76^3/$_4$ × 103^1/$_2$″. Prado, Madrid

11 JAN BRUEGEL THE ELDER. *Taste* from "The Five Senses." Signed on the stool at right: "Brueghel fe. 1618." Panel, 25^1/$_4$ × 42^1/$_2$″. Prado, Madrid

12 JAN BRUEGEL THE ELDER. *Touch* [sic] *(Smell)* from "The Five Senses." Signed at lower right: "Brueghel." Panel, 25^1/$_2$ × 43″. Prado, Madrid

13 JAN BRUEGEL THE ELDER. *Village Street*. Signed at lower right: "Brueghel 1610." Copper, 3^1/$_4$ × 5″. Alte Pinakothek, Munich

14 JAN BRUEGEL THE ELDER. *Outskirts of a Village*. Signed at lower left: "I. Brueghel 1597." Copper, 11^1/$_4$ × 14^1/$_2$″. State Museum of Hesse, Kassel

15 JAN BRUEGEL THE ELDER. *River Scene with Boats and Figures*. Signed at lower left: "Brueghel 1606." Copper, 11^1/$_4$ × 16^3/$_4$″. Wellington Museum, London

16 JAN BRUEGEL THE ELDER. *Jonah's Deliverance from the Whale*. Panel, 15 × 22″. Alte Pinakothek, Munich

17 JAN BRUEGEL THE ELDER. *The Burning of Troy*. Copper, 10^1/$_4$ × 14″. Alte Pinakothek, Munich

18 JAN BRUEGEL THE ELDER and SEBASTIAEN VRANCX. *The Ambush*. Panel, 22 × 33^1/$_2$″. Kunsthistorisches Museum, Vienna

19 JAN BRUEGEL THE ELDER. *Travelers in a Landscape*. Signed at lower right: "Brueghel 1616." Copper, 10 × 14^1/$_2$″. Wellington Museum, London

20 JAN BRUEGEL THE ELDER. *Forest Road by a Riverbank*. Copper, 13 × 18^3/$_4$″. Öffentliche Kunstsammlung, Basel

21 JAN BRUEGEL THE ELDER. *The Earthly Paradise (Earth* from "The Four Elements"). Copper, 18 × 26^1/$_2$″. Louvre, Paris

22 JAN BRUEGEL THE ELDER. *The Garden of Eden*. Copper, 11^1/$_2$ × 15″. Städel Institute, Frankfort

23 PETER PAUL RUBENS and JAN BRUEGEL THE ELDER. *Paradise* (Adam and Eve in the Garden). Signed: "Petri Pauli Rubens Figr. Brueghel Fec." Panel, 29 × 45″. Mauritshuis, The Hague

List of Drawings by Jan Bruegel

(between pages 28-33)

Photo Credits for Black-and-White Illustrations

Bibliography

Bazin, Germain. *Gallery of Flowers*, New York, 1964.

Behling, Lottlisa. *Die Pflanze in der mittelalterlichen Tafelmalerei*, Weimar, 1957.

———. *Die Pflanzenwelt der mittelalterlichen Kathedralen*, Cologne-Graz, 1964.

de Bie, Cornelis. *Het gulden Cabinet vande edel vry schilderconst*, Lier, 1661.

Böhling, Luise. "Blume, Blumenmalerei, Blumenstück," *Reallexikon zur Deutschen Kunstgeschichte*, Stuttgart, 1937 ff.

Brecht, Bertolt. "Verfremdungseffekt in den erzählenden Bildern des älteren Brueghel," *Bildende Kunst*, 1957.

Burger, Fritz. "Die deutsche Malerei vom ausgehenden Mittelalter bis zum Ende der Renaissance," *Handbuch der Kunstwissenschaft*, Vol. I, Berlin, 1913.

Combe, Jacques. *Brueghel de Velours*, Paris, 1942.

Delen, Adrien-Jean-Joseph. *Illustrations de livres par Pierre Coecke d'Alost*, Brussels-Paris, 1931.

Drost, Willy. "Barockmalerei in den germanischen Ländern," *Handbuch der Kunstwissenschaft*, Wildpark-Potsdam, 1929.

Dülberg, Franz. "Niederländische Malerei der Spätgotik und Renaissance," *Handbuch der Kunstwissenschaft*, Wildpark-Potsdam, 1929.

van der Elst, J. *L'Age d'Or flamand*, Paris, 1931.

Friedländer, Max, J. *From Van Eyck to Bruegel*, New York, 1956.

Genaille, Robert. *Die flämische Malerei*, Stuttgart, 1961.

Gerig, Hans. "Vom Beiwerk an Stephan Lochners 'Muttergottes mit dem Veilchen'," *Jahrbuch des kölnischen Geschichtsvereins*, Vol. XXVI, 1951.

Gerson, Horst Karl. "Jan Brueghel der Ältere," *Kindlers Malerei-Lexikon*, Zurich, 1964.

Greindl, E. *Les Peintres flamands de nature morte au XVIIᵉ siècle*, Brussels, 1956.

———. *La Peinture flamande au XVIIᵉ siècle*, Brussels, 1964.

Hairs, Marie-Louise. *Les Peintres flamands de fleurs au XVIIᵉ siècle*, Paris-Brussels, 1965.

Hampp, Irmgard. *Beschwörung Segen Gebet*, Stuttgart, 1961.

Hansmann, Liselotte and Kriss-Rettenbeck, Lenz. *Amulett und Talisman*, Munich, 1966.

Kauffmann, Hans. "Die Fünf Sinne in der niederländischen Malerei des 17. Jahrhunderts," *Kunstgeschichtliche Studien: Festschrift für Dagobert Frey*, ed. by H. Tintelot, Breslau, 1943.

Klauner, Friderike. "Zur Landschaft Jan Brueghels d. Ä.," *Nationalmusei Årsbok 1949–1950*, Stockholm, 1952.

Lassaigne, Jacques and Delevoy, Robert. *Flemish Painting*, Vol. II: *From Bosch to Rubens*, Cleveland, 1958.

von Löhneysen, Hans-Wolfgang. *Die ältere niederländische Malerei. Künstler und Kritiker*, Eisenach-Kassel, 1956.

Pevsner, Nikolaus and Meier, Michael. *Grünewald*, New York, 1958.

van Puyvelde, Leo. *La Peinture flamande à Rome*, Brussels, 1950.

Raczyński, Count Josef Alexander. *Die flämische Landschafts-malerei vor Rubens*, Frankfort, 1937.

Schmitz, Hermann. "Die deutsche Malerei vom ausgehenden Mittelalter bis zum Ende der Renaissance," *Handbuch der Kunstwissenschaft*, Vol. III, Berlin, 1919.

Thiéry, Yvonne. *Le Paysage flamand au XVIIe siècle*, Paris-Brussels, 1953.

Winner, Matthias. "Zeichnungen des älteren Jan Brueghel," *Jahrbuch der Berliner Museen*, Vol. III, 1961.

Index of Names